PREVOST BUSES
1924 THROUGH 2002
PHOTO ARCHIVE

William A. Luke

D1597323

Iconografix
Photo Archive Series

Iconografix
PO Box 446
Hudson, Wisconsin 54016 USA

The information in this book is true and complete to the best of our knowledge. All recommendations are made without any guarantee on the part of the author or Publisher, who also disclaim any liability incurred in connection with the use of this data or specific details.

We acknowledge that certain words, such as model names and designations, mentioned herein are the property of the trademark holder. We use them for purposes of identification only. This is not an official publication.

Iconografix books are offered at a discount when sold in quantity for promotional use. Businesses or organizations seeking details should write to the Marketing Department, Iconografix, at the above address.

Library of Congress Card Number: 2002104775

ISBN 1-58388-083-6

02 03 04 05 06 07 08 5 4 3 2 1

Printed in China

Cover and book design by Shawn Glidden

Copyediting by Suzie Helberg

COVER PHOTO: The Prevost H3-45-2003 is the model introduced early in 2002. It has many new features such as two large windshields, frameless flush-mounted side windows and passenger-friendly entranceway.

BOOK PROPOSALS

Iconografix is a publishing company specializing in books for transportation enthusiasts. We publish in a number of different areas, including Automobiles, Auto Racing, Buses, Construction Equipment, Emergency Equipment, Farming Equipment, Railroads & Trucks. The Iconografix imprint is constantly growing and expanding into new subject areas.

Authors, editors, and knowledgeable enthusiasts in the field of transportation history are invited to contact the Editorial Department at Iconografix, Inc., PO Box 446, Hudson, WI 54016.

Table of contents

ACKNOWLEDGMENTS

Photographs in this book are from the bus history library of the author, William A. Luke, unless noted as photo credits from other individuals and organizations.

The following persons and organizations were very helpful in providing information that has made this book possible:

Jean Breton, Bus Industry Historian, Charlesbourg, Quebec

Tom Jones, Librarian, Motor Bus Society, Clark, New Jersey

Jack D. Knowles, Bus Industry Historian, Toronto, Ontario

Paul A. Leger, President, Bus History Association, Halifax, Nova Scotia

Andre Martineau, Grimm Design, Quebec City, Quebec

Peter Newgard, President, Canadian Transit Heritage Foundation, Gloucester, Ontario

John H. Rieth, Bus Industry Historian, Old Bridge, New Jersey

A special acknowledgment also goes to Paul Leger for the abundance of detailed information about the buses and companies featured in this book, especially those from eastern Canada. Paul provided several excellent photographs as well.

FOREWORD

One of the important items on my agenda in 1999 was our 75th anniversary. We had to somehow pay tribute to the Prevost Car pioneers whose great work over the years had contributed so much to our success. This became more and more obvious to me as I browsed through the company archives.

As luck would have it, I ran into William A. Luke, the "dean" of cross-country bus literature during our 75th anniversary celebration at the UMA Show in Houston. After looking over the Prevost memorabilia exhibit we had on the floor, Bill turned to me and said: "George, this is great stuff. I'm pretty sure I could come up with a photo archive that will bring back plenty of fond memories and show the younger people in the business what it was like way back when."

As we discussed the matter further, reliving some of the many milestones that paved the way for us, I was amazed with Bill's knowledge of our company and how the Prevost product line had evolved over the years. I was soon convinced that Bill was the perfect man to carry out a labor-of-love archive project like this.

Having three-quarters of a century of company history compiled by a world-class expert (on his own time, I might add) is in itself a tribute to the dedication and perseverance of the people who helped make Prevost a leading North American manufacturer of luxury highway coaches and bus shells for conversion.

On behalf of past, present and future employees of Prevost Car, I wish to thank Bill Luke for his personal initiative and dedication in putting this magnificent photo archive together. And as I read through it, I'm also sincerely grateful to the generations of loyal customers who have helped make Prevost Car the major player we are in bus transportation and luxury motor homes today.

George Bourelle
President and Chief Executive Officer
Prevost Car Inc.

www.prevostcar.com

INTRODUCTION

In the small Quebec village of Ste.-Claire, a man named Eugene Prevost had a shop where he built furniture and cabinetry. Prevost began this venture in 1915, and his quality workmanship was well received.

It was a chilly, snowy Quebec winter in 1924 when a friend, George Roy, approached Prevost and asked him to build a passenger-carrying body on a newly purchased Reo truck chassis. The result was the first Prevost bus.

This was the beginning of today's Prevost Car, Inc., a leading builder of luxury motor coaches and conversion shells for specialized vehicles.

Prevost Car has had a rich history and from the early days it has built a variety of buses, motor coaches and conversion shells. Current Prevost motor coaches and specialized vehicles are seen everywhere throughout the United States and Canada.

After Eugene Prevost built that first bus, he continued building buses on a small scale while he kept building furniture. He limited bus building to one bus each winter. But the demand for buses grew, and a bus manufacturing plant was built in 1937. Growth in the business made plant additions necessary, and by 1947 the Prevost manufacturing complex was 22,000 square feet.

The first Prevost buses were built on truck chassis. Chassis from White Motor Company were favored in most cases, but some Prevost bus bodies were built on Reo, Fargo, Maple Leaf and other chassis from popular truck manufacturers. Some stretched-out sedans were also built.

The bus bodies, made of wood, were strong but heavy. These wooden bodies nevertheless proved satisfactory in their day. In the 1930s wood frames were continued, but metal became the material of choice for the side panels.

After World War II buses were in great demand, keeping the Prevost factory very busy. The company was incorporated in 1947 as Les Ateliers Prevost, and the plant was expanded to nearly 40,000 square feet—about twice its previous size.

Prevost built both intercity coaches and transit and suburban buses through the 1950s. Despite the demise of many bus manufacturers in North America at that time, Prevost was able to survive. However, production of city and suburban buses was de-emphasized.

A name change took place in 1957 when the Normand interest, a family of industrialists, became the new owners of the company. The name became Prevost Car, Inc. Around that time, Prevost began building rear-engined buses, debuting a modern-style bus called the Le Normand. It also had air suspension, diesel power and other new features.

The Prevost Panoramique was introduced in 1962. Although most of the Panoramiques were two-axle models, some were longer and had three axles, large side windows, improved air suspension and other enhancements.

In 1967, the Prevost Champion, first shown at the National Association of Motor Bus Owners (NAMBO) annual meeting in Montreal, marked another advancement in Prevost coach design. The Champion was greeted with high interest, including that of bus operators in the United States. Prior to this time Prevost buses had only been marketed in Canada.

The interest in the United States was great enough that a sales and service network was established. The first sales and service facility in the United States was in Lyndhurst, New Jersey. Somerset Bus Company of Somerset, New Jersey was the first American operator to acquire a new Prevost coach.

The bus industry in the United States and Canada was experiencing a growth in bus tourism. Many companies were emerging and were devoted only to operating tours. Regular-route bus companies were also devoting more resources to tourism. Prevost recognized this and developed the Prestige coach in 1973. It had side windows extending into the roof of the coach, giving passengers greater viewing opportunities. The Prestige was in great demand by many companies. Also in 1973, Prevost expanded its plant by 35,000 square feet. In 1976, the Le Mirage coach—patterned after the Prestige—was unveiled.

Prevost also saw an opportunity in offering the Le Mirage without seats and other interior finishing. There were a number of firms specializing in finishing the interiors of coaches as luxurious motor homes for individuals, entertainers and others. Various corporations also found the Prevost Le Mirage conversion coaches could be made into coaches for display and other purposes. The conversion coach market became important for Prevost.

A new 100,000-square-foot Prevost plant was built in 1980 on a 10-acre site not far from the original plant in Ste.-Claire. It had the most modern equipment, including a transboarder system; a conveyor system that enables coaches in most stages of production to be moved to positions for specialized work or for further production. This gave the Prevost plant greater flexibility.

In 1984, when legislation allowed wider buses, Prevost introduced the 102-inch-wide Marathon XL and Le Mirage XL buses. Conversion shells were also available with wider bodies.

Prevost Car invested considerably in research and development. A result of this was the H5-60, launched in late 1985. The spectacular new 60-foot articulated bus had five axles with two steering axles in the front, and a seating capacity of 72 passengers. A Detroit Diesel 8V-92 diesel engine was mounted in the center of the front section.

The styling and many of the features of the H5-60 were incorporated in the H3-40 coach, introduced in 1990. When legislation allowed for 45-foot buses, the 56-passenger H3-45 model was launched. The H3-41 coach was later added to succeed the H3-40.

The increased length for non-articulated buses gave Prevost the opportunity to lengthen the Le Mirage XL coach, and a new 45-foot Le Mirage XL was made available.

All the H-series Prevost coaches and the Le Mirage were offered as conversions for luxury motor homes and specialty vehicles. This part of Prevost's business has continued to increase.

Another important Prevost milestone took place in 1995. The company was acquired jointly by Sweden's Volvo Bus Corporation and Henlys Group plc of the United Kingdom. This infused Prevost Car with new capital, which was used for new equipment and production expansion. Parts and services facilities were also expanded.

A facelift was given to the popular Le Mirage XL coach in 1999, and the new-look Le Mirage, a 45-foot coach, became known as the Le Mirage XL II.

With Prevost approaching its 80th anniversary in 2004, the H-series coaches have undergone a number of changes. These include a new full-height, two-piece windshield; flush-mounted side windows and a passenger-friendly entrance.

Prevost has also achieved three ISO (International Organization for Standardization) certifications: ISO 9001 for overall quality processes, ISO 9002 for aftermarket processes, and ISO 14001 for environmental management.

Not only has Prevost Car demonstrated orderly growth throughout its rich history, but the company also shows a strong commitment to continued strength, ensuring future success.

Early Prevost Buses

Eugene Prevost was challenged by his long-time friend, George Roy, to build a bus body on the new 1924 Reo truck chassis Roy had purchased. This wooden bus body on the chassis became the first Prevost bus. Prevost continued building one bus each winter until demand resulted in the launching of a bus building shop in 1937.

A large Cadillac sedan of mid-1930 vintage was stretched out by Eugene Prevost for an unknown bus operator in Quebec. It is pictured here in front of the factory, which was built in 1939 in Ste.-Claire. Although most of the early Prevost buses were bodies on truck chassis, this represented another type of bus that Prevost was able to build in the early days. There was a significant demand for stretched-out buses in the 1930s.

Arthur J. Dumais, Jr. and Brothers of Lewiston, Maine had Prevost extend the body of a Pierce-Arrow sedan in 1936; the stretched-out result is shown here. It was reportedly the first Prevost vehicle bought by a bus operator in the United States. The Dumais bus line—which operated between Lewiston and Levis, Quebec—was a short-lived operation, beginning in 1938 and folding a year later.

10

Prevost built a number of stretched-out buses that were originally sedans or station wagons. This 1936 Dodge stretch-out pictured at the original Prevost factory in Ste.-Claire, Quebec, went into service for Autobus Fournier as its No. 4 bus. Autobus Fournier was a large bus operator located in the Quebec City suburb of Ste.-Foy. *Paul A. Leger*

This 37-passenger Prevost bus was built on a White chassis. It was owned by Lamothe Coach Lines, which operated between Noranda and Waite-Armulet Mines in northwestern Quebec. This Prevost bus was reportedly delivered in 1944.

Autobus Ile d'Orleans, Limitee, founded in 1924 by Ozea Gagnon, operated around the island and service to Quebec City began in 1935 when a bridge was built. Gagnon sold the line to G. Vaillancourt in 1947. In 1971, the line was again sold and became D'Autobus Ile d'Orleans, Limitee. Then in 1983 the Ile d'Orleans bus services ended. The original owner of the bus service bought the Prevost bus pictured here in 1940. It had a White chassis.

This shows the framework of a new Prevost bus built in the early 1940s. The framework was constructed in one part of the Prevost plant, then pushed across the street for the body to be completed with a metal skin.

Autobus St.-Zacharie was a small bus company that operated a route between St.-Zacharie, near the Quebec-Maine border, and Levis, Quebec, across the St. Lawrence River from Quebec City. This 1940 Prevost mounted on a White chassis was used on the route. This particular model had unusual front fenders.

Levis Transport Company of Levis, Quebec, was the successor of Levis Tramways, Ltd., which operated urban service in the Levis, Quebec area. Eight of these Prevost Suburban buses were purchased in 1944, and seven similar buses were added in 1945. These buses were built on GMC chassis. *Paul A. Leger*

Carier & Frere, Ltd., Shawinigan Falls, Quebec, acquired this 15-passenger Dodge Utility vehicle that Prevost stretched to create a bus in 1948. Carier & Frere operated city service in the Shawinigan area and also had suburban service in the Trois Rivieres area. The company also had routes from its service area to and from Montreal that started in 1946, and later to and from Quebec City. The bus company was founded in 1922 by Theodore Carier. *Paul A. Leger*

Early Prevost Factory Views

The original Prevost plant is shown in this aerial view. The large addition at the rear of the three-section plant in the front was added in 1947. The building in the upper left of this view was built in 1951. The buildings in the immediate foreground were demolished about 1960, although the two bottom left buildings are still up.

This is a view of the assembly line in the Prevost factory in Ste.-Claire, Quebec, circa 1950. It shows one of the Interurban models along with two City buses. In the background are frames for Interurban models.

This custom-built Prevost Interurban model was delivered to Service d'Autobus Thetford Mines (Quebec). It had two doors, accommodated 37 passengers and had a Continental gasoline engine mounted in the rear. Service d'Autobus Thetford Mines served the mining districts in south central Quebec.

Gloucester Motor Coach Line of Bathurst, New Brunswick was established in 1927, operating a route on the New Brunswick Caraquet Coast between Bathurst and Tracadie. Shown here is one of three Prevost Interurban coaches owned by the company.

Maple Leaf Lines was the trade name of a bus service operated by Cecil Norton of Burlington, Ontario. Norton bought the company in 1956 from Oakville Transportation Co. This 1949 Prevost Interurban was in the fleet when Norton acquired the company.

Bluebird Coach Lines of Woodstock, Ontario, operated this Prevost 33-passenger Interurban model. Bluebird had seven Prevost intercity coaches of 1949-1950 vintage, as well as two Prevost transit buses. The company operated town service in Woodstock. There were also a number of intercity routes in the Woodstock, Ingersoll, and London areas. The Prevost pictured, powered by an International Super Red Diamond gasoline engine, was acquired by Eastern Canadian Greyhound Lines of Toronto, Ontario in 1951.

Airline Limousines, Ltd., of Montreal, Quebec, purchased this 33-passenger Prevost Skycruiser in July 1949. This was the only coach owned by the company, which carried passengers between Montreal's Dorval Airport and the city. Murray Hill Taxis, Ltd. of Montreal bought Airline Limousines and this coach.

Frontenac Coach Lines of Kingston, Ontario bought this Prevost intercity bus in 1950. The company operated a country route from Kingston to Harrowsmith, Verona, Parkham and Shabot Lake. This model Prevost had seats for 37 passengers and had an International Red Diamond 6-cylinder gasoline engine mounted in the rear. *J.D. Knowles*

Autobus Sorel-Ste.-Angele Ltd. of Nicolet, Quebec, began in 1945 with three daily trips between Sorel and Ste.-Angele. In 1949, service was extended on a route between Sorel and Montreal. Later, a local service was begun serving Quebec City as well as communities along the St. Lawrence River's south shore. In 1962, the name was changed to Les Autobus de la Rive Sud. The new name appears on this 1949 Prevost Interurban bus when it was pictured in 1967. The company had four of these buses.

Roseland Bus Lines was an early suburban charter bus operator in the Roseland area of Toronto, Ontario. This 33-passenger Prevost Interurban coach was purchased in 1953 and used in Roseland's charter service. The company also had two Prevost transit buses and another Prevost intercity bus. Roseland was taken over by the Toronto Transit Commission and its subsidiary Gray Coach Lines, Ltd. in 1954.

Autobus Lemelin, Ltee of Quebec City, purchased the Prevost Prevocar pictured here in 1953. The Prevocar model followed the Prevost Interurban. It had the same body but with some changes such as the longer side windows. Autobus Lemelin began in 1927 with a route between Levis and Ste.-Anne de la Pocatiere. The route was extended to Rimouski in 1941 and eventually to Edmundston, New Brunswick. Lemelin sold the routes to Voyageur in March 1965.

Autobus Fournier, Ltd., Ste.-Foy, Quebec, added this Prevost Interurban in 1951. It was a 44-passenger bus, the largest produced by Prevost at the time. Autobus Fournier operated suburban bus services in the Quebec City area and also had an important intercity route between Quebec City and the Lac St.-Jean area in northern Quebec.

These two Prevost 37-passenger intercity coaches had three owners and are shown in the livery of the third owner, Murray Hill Limousine Service of Montreal, Quebec. Bluebird Coach Lines of Woodstock, Ontario originally purchased them in 1948, and when Bluebird was sold to Eastern Canadian Greyhound Lines in 1951 the coaches were added to the Eastern Canadian fleet. Murray Hill rebuilt the coaches and installed glass windows on the top.

In 1951, Les Ateliers Prevost displayed this new Interurban coach at the Association des Proprietaires d'Autobus du Quebec convention in Montreal. Left to right are: Albert Lacombe, sales manager; Louis Bilodeau, associate, and Eugene Prevost, founder of the Prevost company.

Diamond Bus Lines of Edmonton, Alberta operated suburban bus service in the Edmonton area beginning in 1949. The first bus was a 1949 Prevost Suburban with a Hercules JXLD 6-cylinder gasoline engine mounted in the rear. Three more Prevost transit buses were acquired by Diamond the following year. The owner, Cecil Bradshaw, later became the Western Canadian sales representative for Prevost.

Excel Coach Lines of Kenora, Ontario, bought this Prevost Transit in 1950. It had a Hercules JXLD 6-cylinder engine mounted in the rear. Excel Coach Lines, which began serving the area in 1934, operated the Cityliner on a route between Kenora and nearby Keewatin.

The Guelph (Ontario) Transportation Commission purchased five 41-passenger Prevost Transit buses in 1954. They were powered with Leyland diesel engines. The four Prevost buses operated for 16 years in urban service in the Guelph area.

Pictou County Bus Services of New Glasgow, Nova Scotia operated this 1950 Prevost intercity bus in suburban service. It had a Ford chassis and engine. The bus was acquired second-hand from Clairie's Bus and Taxi Company of Truro, Nova Scotia. Pictou County Bus Services, originally known as Pictou County Electric Company Limited (the name was changed in 1952), first operated buses in 1926. The Irving interests in New Brunswick bought the company in 1987.

Owned by Ed Carter, Local Lines Ltd. of Sudbury, Ontario acquired this 1958 Prevost intercity bus from the Canadian Army in 1964. Local Lines Ltd. was one of several small bus lines that operated city and local intercity service in the Sudbury area until the Sudbury Transit System was formed in 1976. *J.D. Knowles*

In 1951-1952, Prevost built the cab-over-engine transit/suburban bus, which seated 29 passengers. It had a transit-type door behind the front wheels. This Prevost transit was operated by Autobus Montmagny (Quebec), Inc.

In 1960, Montreal-based Murray Hill Limousine Service, Ltd. was looking for a new type of bus to replace stretched Chrysler sedans used in airport service between Montreal and Dorval Airport. Murray Hill and Prevost engineers designed this 19-passenger bus, named the Travel Air. It was built on a GMC 3500 chassis. Murray Hill purchased 20 of these buses in 1961. *Paul A. Leger*

British Columbia Hydro was the bus operator in the Vancouver, British Columbia area in the 1960s. In 1965, the company needed buses to serve the new Simon Fraser University campus. It was a difficult high-capacity route with a 16 percent grade. Prevost was asked to build the 45-passenger, 40-foot buses. An 8-cylinder Detroit Diesel engine and manual transmission was used for the buses. Pictured is one of the five buses delivered by Prevost to British Columbia Hydro in 1965. *Paul A. Leger*

The first of 29 Le Normand model Prevost buses was this one acquired by Autobus Ste.-Claire Ste.-Justine St.-Narcisse, Ltee. of Quebec City in 1957. This bus had an International Red Diamond gasoline engine in the rear and seated 37 passengers. George Roy purchased the Autobus Ste.-Claire Ste.-Justine St.-Narcisse company's original route in 1922, and after a series of extensions Ste.-Justine became the terminus of the line in 1932. The company was sold in 1949 to Messrs Beaudet and Gingras, who sold it to Transport Fontaine in 1972.

This forward-mounted 33-passenger Prevost Le Normand bus was delivered to Autobus Drolet Ltee of Ancienne Lorette, Quebec in 1958. It had a General Motors 671 gasoline engine. The company operated a number of local routes in the Quebec City area. This bus was the second Le Normand built.

The Prevost Le Normand was introduced in 1957. Some changes to the style of the Le Normand were made by the time this bus was acquired in 1960 by Archambault & Fils, Inc., La Providence (St.-Hyacinthe), Quebec. A.J. Archambault founded Archambault & Fils in 1929 with a route operating between St.-Hyacinthe and St.-Denis. The company was sold to Bonin Autobus, Ltd. of Sorel, Quebec in 1972.

Prevost Car, Inc. introduced the Le Normand coach in 1960. It seated 41 passengers and it was the first Prevost to have air suspension and a Detroit Diesel engine. Travelways of Toronto, Ontario acquired this Le Normand coach from Frontenac Coach Lines of Kingston, Ontario. *J.D. Knowles*

This Prevost Le Normand coach was acquired by Autobus Sorel-Ste.-Angele, Ltd. of Nicolet, Quebec in 1961. It was a 37-passenger model and featured a gradual sloping floor extending the full length of the coach, giving passengers an excellent forward view. This Le Normand had a General Motors 6V-71 diesel engine.

This 1961 Prevost Transit model bus was originally a school bus demonstrator and outfitted with seats for 74 children. It was an attempt by Prevost to enter the school bus market, but only two buses of this model were built. Autobus La Malbaie bought this bus, which was powered by a rear-mounted General Motors gasoline engine.

Panoramique Models

Autobus Drummondville (Quebec) purchased five of these Prevost Panoramique buses in 1962. They were 45-passenger models, powered by General Motors 671 gasoline engines. Autobus Drummondville operated a number of urban and intercity routes in the area, including the important Montreal-Drummondville route.

Grey Goose Bus Lines Ltd., a pioneer Manitoba bus line headquartered in Winnipeg, acquired three 49-S Prevost Panoramique buses beginning in 1962. This one, with a General Motors 6V-71 diesel engine, joined the fleet in 1963.

In 1968, the Canadian National Railways discontinued train service across the province of Newfoundland after the opening of the Trans-Canada Highway. This Prevost I-41 bus and eight TS-47 Prevost buses were utilized in Newfoundland on the Port aux Basque-St. John's service.

C.H. Norton Bus Lines, Ltd. (d.b.a. The Maple Leaf Way) operated this 1961 Prevost I-49 in its extensive tour and charter service. Though it was sold to Travelways in 1974, the company had operated independently. *J.D. Knowles*

This 1962 Prevost Panoramique coach was owned by Wagar Coach Lines of Napanee, Ontario. The company began in 1930 running rural service, and in later years charters and tours were operated. In 1976, Wagar Coach merged with Trentway Bus Lines to form Trentway-Wagar, Inc., an important Ontario bus company. *J.D. Knowles*

The Prevost I-47 Panoramique was built in 1967 and delivered to Les Autobus Deshaies Ltee of Deschaillons, Quebec. This bus was used on an express route between Levis, Quebec and Montreal and this service was announced on the sides of the bus. It was unusual because it had the body of a Prevost Champion but the front of the Panoramique.

This 35-foot Prevost Panoramique of 1972 was one of the earlier conversion coaches built by Prevost. The coach had a number of options, such as the different window arrangements shown here. The interiors could be completed in many different arrangements to suit a private individual for a motor home, or a corporation for display and for guests.

Prevost's Champion model was first produced in 1966. It had a new structural design with extra-large windows for enhanced passenger viewing. This model was first shown at the American Bus Association's annual meeting in Montreal in 1967, and was introduced to bus operators in the United States soon after. Detroit Diesel's 8V-71 engine and Spicer's 8844-A 4-speed direct-drive transmission were standard.

The interior of the Prevost factory in 1967, showing Champion models on the assembly line. The body on the left had received flooring and side panels were being installed. The body on the right was being inspected.

54

The first large Prevost coach to be sold in the United States was this TS-4776 model. It was the first of four similar Prevost coaches purchased by Somerset Bus Company of Mountainside, New Jersey. Reg Krug's Truck & Bus Import Corporation was responsible for this sale in the spring of 1968. It was the start of continuous sales of Prevost coaches by many bus companies in the United States. This Somerset Prevost coach is pictured at the Canadian border as it crossed into the United States.

Pontiac Bus Lines, Ltd. of Campbell's Bay, Quebec purchased this 47-passenger Prevost TS-47 in April 1973. Pontiac Bus Lines had its beginning in 1940 and operated employee service between Campbell's Bay and New Calumet Mines. Later, the company began a route between Ottawa, Ontario and Fort-Coulonge, Quebec via Campbell's Bay. *Peter Newgard*

Autobus C. Monette & Fils of Delson, Quebec bought this 102-inch-wide Prevost TS-47 in 1968. Since Monette & Fils first began it has been a loyal Prevost customer; one of its first Prevost buses was a Prevocar. No longer in business, Autobus C. Monette & Fils was primarily a school bus operator but also had commuter and charter services.

Canadian National Railways, which began operating bus service across the province of Newfoundland, added eight of these Prevost Champion Model TS-47 coaches in 1969. These buses joined 12 Model I-41 Prevost buses, which entered service in 1968 for Canadian National when the Newfoundland rail service was discontinued.

The origins of Autobus Drolet, Ltd. date to 1916. At that time Napoleon Drolet operated a local bus company in the Quebec City area. The company was incorporated in 1932, and in 1945 it began a 200-mile route along the North Shore of the St. Lawrence River serving Baie-Comeau and Forestville. Suburban service in the Quebec City area began in 1969. The North Shore route was bought by Voyageur in 1976. This Prevost Champion TS-102 was bought by Drolet in 1973.

R. Helfrich & Son Corporation of East Keansburg, New Jersey, was one of 17 bus companies in that state, which bought the first Prevost Champion buses when they were introduced in the United States. Pictured here is the 1976 Champion acquired by Helfrich. It has a Detroit Diesel 8V-71 engine, a 6-speed manual transmission, lavatory, and 51 seats (two rows had been added). It is still owned by Helfrich and operated in the company's charter service. The Helfrich company began in 1931 as a school bus operator and in the early 1960s it began charter and tour service. *John D. Rieth*

This Pacific Western Transportation, Ltd. Prevost Prestige bus and four others were delivered in 1976. The company had also received two similar Prestige coaches the year before. Calgary, Alberta-based Pacific Western began January 1, 1961, as a holding company.

CTCUM is the French-language abbreviation for the Montreal (Quebec) Urban Community Transport Commission. In 1975, 30 of these Prevost Prestige buses were purchased for service between downtown Montreal and Mirabel and Dorval airports. CTCUM was a Gray Line Sight-Seeing Association member at the time, and these buses were used occasionally for sight-seeing service.

In this 1968 Prevost factory view, new Prestige models were under construction. These were the first models to have the high side windows.

Prevost Car has always been known to adapt to customers' special needs. This Prevost Prestige model with a center door was delivered to the Congregation Yetev Lev in New York City in 1977. The center door was specified to allow women and men to each have their own entrance and exit door, it was reported.

In 1987, Voyageur, Inc. of Montreal, Quebec purchased 40 Prevost Le Mirage XL model coaches for intercity routes operating throughout the province of Quebec. Voyageur, which began operating bus service in 1927, was formerly known as Provincial Transport Company.

This was the first new Prevost Le Mirage delivered to Murray Hill Limousine Service in Montreal, Quebec. It was added to the fleet for service between Montreal and the city's Dorval Airport. Murray Hill Limousines got its start by transferring passengers from the upstart Trans-Canada Airline in 1934 at St.-Hubert. Limousines were initially used, but buses replaced the limousines as air travel increased. Prevost buses were chosen to provide the transportation for Murray Hill air passengers.

In 1985, Prevost offered the Astral XL coach, featuring roof windows designed for bus companies offering sight-seeing services. Pacific Western Transportation Company of Calgary, Alberta, bought six of these sight-seeing coaches. This Prevost Astral XL coach is pictured in Banff National Park with the Banff Springs Hotel in the background. Pacific Western has been a large customer of Prevost coaches for many years. Total production of the Astral XL model was 12 units. *Brian Grams*

This photo shows the interior of the Astral XL coach Prevost introduced in 1985. The roof windows gave passengers a greater opportunity for sight-seeing, especially in mountain areas. Only 12 of the Astral XL coaches—which were based on a Prevost Le Mirage body—were built. *Brian Grams*

When 102-inch-wide buses were made legal in North America in 1984, Prevost Car responded by increasing the width of the two models being produced at the time. They were referred to as XL models. The Prevost XL, primarily an intercity route coach called the Marathon, is pictured here. A Detroit Diesel 8V-92 engine was mounted in the rear.

This is an aerial view of the new Prevost factory built in 1980. It was located on a 10-acre site in the village of Ste.-Claire, not far from the original Prevost plant. The new plant covered 100,000 square feet and featured a conveyor (transboarder) in the center aisle. This allowed buses in production to be easily moved to positions for specialized attention or for further production or painting.

In late 1985, Prevost Car, Inc. introduced the H5-60, a revolutionary articulated intercity coach. The coach has five axles including twin steering axles in the front. The H5-60 is 60 feet long, 102 inches wide and 144 inches high. Normal seating is 71 passengers. A Detroit Diesel 8V-92 DDEC diesel engine is mounted in the middle of the front section.

This Prevost H5-60 articulated coach was one of 12 that entered service for Voyageur in 1988. These coaches had special two-and-one seating for 51 passengers and were used on Voyageur's Montreal-Quebec City route. Voyageur sold the Montreal-Quebec City route to Autocars Orleans Express. These coaches have since been sold by Autocars Orleans Express.

In 1991, Holland America Line-Westours of Seattle, Washington, took delivery of 14 Prevost H5-60 coaches for touring on the Alaska Highway in Alaska and the Yukon. The coaches were referred to as the Alaska Yukon Explorer. Lounge Coach Special was the seating featured with a lounge configuration in the rear. The coaches had galleys at the rear and a lavatory. Holland America-Westours took delivery of three more H5-60 coaches one year later.

The Prevost H3-40 was introduced in January 1990 at the United Bus Owners of America Bus Expo in Dallas, Texas. Its design came from the Prevost H5-60 articulated bus of 1985, but a number of technology improvements were made. The 40-foot coach offered a Detroit Diesel 6V-92 DDEC 300-horsepower engine as standard, and a larger 400-horsepower Detroit Diesel 8V-92 DDEC as an option.

The interior of the Prevost H3-40 coach had seats for 48 passengers. The large windows gave passengers an outstanding opportunity to view scenery as they traveled. This resulted in the immediate popularity of this Prevost model by tour and charter bus companies. There were many options to add to the comfort and convenience of passengers.

Autobus Orleans Express of Quebec City, Quebec, was formed in 1990 to assume the routes vacated by Voyageur in Quebec. This Prevost H3-40 was a former demonstrator built in 1993. In addition, this particular bus also operated for Voyageur Colonial on Quebec-Ontario routes. In 1999, the bus was sold to Autobus Dupont. Orleans Express has been an important user of Prevost coaches.

Academy Bus Tours of Hoboken, New Jersey, acquired its first Prevost coach in 1992 and added this H3-40 in 1994. Academy had a number of Prevost coaches in its fleet, including 30 Model H3-40 coaches (similar to the one pictured here), 45 Model H3-41 coaches and several Model H3-45s.

Honolulu-based Polynesian Hospitality is an important bus company providing a variety of transportation services to tourists in Hawaii. The company has been a Prevost customer for many years and has approximately 50 Prevost coaches in its fleet, including this Model H3-40 decorated in a special Hawaiian style.

Turner Coaches, Inc. of Terre Haute, Indiana, became an important Prevost customer in recent years. The first Prevost bought by Turner was a Le Mirage XL in 1991. The following year, this Model H3-40 Prevost was acquired. The company also has a 45-foot Prevost Le Mirage XL and four Model H3-45 Prevost coaches. Founded in 1921, Turner Coaches is one of Indiana's pioneer bus companies and has an extensive charter and tour business.

Mid-American Coaches of Washington, Missouri, has several Prevost units including this Model H3-41, acquired with another similar coach in 1996. Two Prevost H3-45s and an H5-60 are in the Mid-American fleet. Mid-American's long bus industry history began in 1927. It is now a leading charter and tour operator in eastern Missouri.

Prevost Car, Inc. celebrated its 70th anniversary in 1994 by introducing the H3-45 coach. The new authorized 45-foot length for intercity coaches prompted Prevost to present the new vehicle. Not only did the new coach feature the added length, but it also had many other innovations. Its popularity was immediately realized.

The Prevost H3-45 coach first presented in 1994 featured a Detroit Diesel 12.7-liter, 400-horsepower DDEC III Series 60 engine. Prevost engineers designed the engine compartment for easy accessibility as noted in this photo. Because of the coach's greater length, more components could be positioned at the rear of the vehicle.

Greyhound Canada Transportation purchased 11 Prevost H3-45 coaches in 1995. They operate mainly on the Toronto-Ottawa route. Greyhound Canada also had a Prevost Le Mirage XL 45 that was generally used on routes operating in the Windsor, Ontario area. These Prevost coaches were the first to be acquired by Greyhound in Canada.

Johnson Bus Company, Elizabethtown, Pennsylvania, purchased this Prevost H3-45 coach in 2000. Johnson, which began in 1939, has an important tour and charter service in the area.

In 1999, Cardinal Buses, Inc., Middlebury, Indiana, added this Prevost H3-45 coach and three others to its fleet. Cardinal has favored Prevost coaches for many years. The company has a rich history, having had its start as a rural passenger and mail service in 1923.

Le Mirage XL 45 Models

Bill Rohrbaugh's Charter Service of Manchester, Maryland has been a Prevost customer for many years. The company's entire fleet of 19 coaches are Prevosts. Pictured is one of the two 45-foot Prevost Le Mirage XL coaches added to the fleet in 1997. The Rohrbaugh company has been in business for 30 years and has been an important charter and tour bus service.

Prevost introduced the Le Mirage XL II at the United Motorcoach Association Bus Expo in Orlando, Florida in January 2000. This 45-foot coach incorporated the design of the previous Le Mirage and Le Mirage XL coaches that had long been in service for bus owners throughout the United States and Canada. The 55-passenger Le Mirage XL II has a Detroit Diesel Series 60 engine and an Allison World 6-speed automatic transmission.

Jefferson Lines of Minneapolis, Minnesota bought five Prevost Le Mirage XL II coaches, with the first being delivered in 1999, two in 2000 and two more in 2001. Jefferson Lines also acquired 11 Le Mirage XL II models and three H3-45 models. Founded in 1919 in Minnesota, Jefferson Lines is one of the state's pioneer bus companies. It has expanded over the years and now operates in 10 states and Canada.

A full-length two-piece front windshield, frameless flush-mounted side windows and a passenger-friendly entranceway were among the new features on the H-series Prevost coaches introduced in 2002. The new coach is pictured here prior to being displayed at the United Motorcoach Association's January 2002 Motorcoach Expo in Indianapolis. The engine for the new coach is a Detroit Diesel Series 60 diesel.

Wolf's Bus Line, York Springs, Pennsylvania, acquired one of the first Prevost H3-45 2003 models shortly after it was introduced in early 2002. This new model has many new features including the large windshield. Wolf's has been a Prevost customer for many years and has 11 Prevost coaches including one of the Prevost XL II coaches.

Autobus P. Heneault of Victoriaville, Quebec operates charter and tour service under the name Bois-Francs. The company bought this 47-passenger Prevost Le Mirage in 1983.

Anchorage-based Alaska Sightseeing Tours acquired three Prevost Le Mirage coaches in 1984. The company, founded by Charles West in 1973, was one of the first bus companies to offer sight-seeing tours in Alaska.

91

In 1985, Gray Line of Seattle (Washington) bought two Prevost Le Mirage XL coaches for sight-seeing, charter and tour service in the Pacific Northwest.

Capitol Bus Company of Harrisburg, Pennsylvania purchased this Prevost Le Mirage XL coach in 1990. Capitol, a member of the Trailways organization, operates route service in eastern Pennsylvania as well as to and from Baltimore and Washington. Capitol began in 1932.

Although the name Bourgeois appears on this Prevost Le Mirage XL coach, it was actually owned by Autobus Drummondville (Quebec), Ltd. The coach was acquired in 1981. Bourgeois is the family name associated with Autobus Drummondville.

This Prevost Le Mirage XL coach is one of six coaches added to the Intercar Saguenay, Ltd. fleet between 1991 and 1995. Intercar Saguenay is headquartered in Jonquiere, Quebec.

Nationwide Travelers of Appleton, Wisconsin acquired this Le Mirage XL in 1995. Nationwide Travelers began in 1974 as a travel club and is now an important charter and tour company with a fleet of 16 Prevost coaches.

Colonial Trailways of Mobile, Alabama acquired two Prevost Le Mirage XL coaches (one pictured here) in 1990. Colonial Trailways, which began in 1935, operates intercity bus routes in the South and also operates charter and tour services.

DRL Coachlines Ltd. became the new bus company to operate service across the province of Newfoundland in 1996. One of its first buses was this 1992 Prevost H3-40 coach leased from 2423-9378 Quebec, Inc. Canadian National Roadcruiser bus service formerly operated the Newfoundland route.

This Prevost Model H3-40 joined the Autocars Jasmin, Inc. fleet in 1992. Autocars Jasmin is a part of the Intercar Group. Founded in 1990, Intercar is headquartered in Jonquiere, Quebec and operates intercity, charter and tour service in the area.

In August 1991, Grey Goose Bus Lines of Winnipeg, Manitoba took delivery of two Prevost Model H3-40 coaches. They were assigned to Grey Goose routes between Winnipeg and northern Manitoba.

Winnipeg-based Beaver Bus Lines has served the Winnipeg and Manitoba region for more than 60 years. The company purchased this Prevost H3-40, one of several coaches in the Beaver Bus Lines fleet, in 1993. This particular unit is assigned to Webb Bus Lines, a Beaver subsidiary.

Lamers Bus Line of Green Bay, Wisconsin bought its first Prevost coach in 1979. This Prevost H3-40 coach was acquired in 1992. Lamers, one of the leading charter and tour operators in the Midwest, has approximately 35 Prevost coaches in its fleet.

Annett Bus Lines of Sebring, Florida, bought this Prevost H3-40 and one other in 1993. Annett is a major charter and tour company in southern Florida.

National Coach Works of Fredericksburg, Virginia bought this Prevost H3-41 in 1995. In addition to operating charter and tour service, National Coach Works is also a used-coach dealer and operates a coach repair facility. It is part of the Martz Group.

All West Coachlines of Sacramento, California has been a loyal Prevost customer for many years. Pictured is one of All West's Prevost H3-40 coaches.

Banff, Alberta-based Brewster Transport Co., which celebrated 100 years in 1992, acquired 16 Prevost H3-45 coaches—including this one—in 1998. Brewster is the pioneer sight-seeing company of the Canadian Rockies.

The Murray Hill division is one of the companies of Groupe Gaudreault in Repentigny, Quebec. Groupe Gaudreault has many Prevost coaches, including this H3-40. There are five other similar coaches in the fleet.

Since it was established in 1987, Cavalier Coach Co. of Boston, Massachusetts has had a number of Prevost coaches in its fleet. Cavalier acquired this Prevost Le Mirage XL in 1996.

Autobus Maheux, Inc. of LaSarre, Quebec bought this 45-foot Prevost XL 45 coach in 1995. The Maheux company operates a variety of services in northern Quebec and has 22 Prevosts in its fleet. *Paul A. Leger*

This Prevost Le Mirage XL II coach was displayed at the Trailways 60th Anniversary Convention in Point Clear, Alabama in 2001.

Newton's Bus Service of Gloucester, Virginia has only Prevost coaches in its 22-vehicle fleet. Two of the 22, including the one pictured, are Prevost Le Mirage XL II models acquired in 2001. These new Prevost coaches have stainless steel on the lower half of the body. *John D. Reith*

SMT (Eastern) Ltd., Dieppe, New Brunswick, acquired two Prevost Le Mirage XL II coaches in 2001. Launched in 1938, SMT operates intercity routes throughout New Brunswick as well as charter and tour services. *Peter Newgard*

Autocars Orleans Express of Montreal, Quebec received 12 Prevost Le Mirage XL II coaches in 2001. These 52-passenger coaches are used on the Montreal-Quebec City route as well as on other Orleans Express routes. *Paul A. Leger*

Nine Prevost H3-41 coaches were purchased by Trentway-Wagar of Peterborough, Ontario in 1995 and were used primarily for charters and tours. Now a Coach Canada company, Trentway-Wagar also has important intercity routes in Ontario and to Montreal, Quebec.

Autocars Connaisseur, Inc. of Quebec City leases this Prevost H3-45 coach and eight others for Gray Line Sight-Seeing service in the Montreal area. Autocars Connaisseur is also a Coach Canada company.

Burke International Tours of Maiden, North Carolina, is also known as Christian Tours. This Prevost Model H3-45 coach and three others were acquired in 1997. Burke International Tours began in 1975 and bought its first Prevost coaches in 1982.

Perkiomen Valley Bus Co. of Pennsburg, Pennsylvania, was a pioneer eastern Pennsylvania bus company that originated in 1925. Perkiomen has been a loyal Prevost customer, purchasing this H3-45 and one other in 1997 along with an H3-41.

Indian Trails of Owosso, Michigan, a pioneer intercity bus company in that state, purchased this Prevost H3-45 coach along with one other in 1998 to add to the six it acquired the previous year. Indian Trails also added five Prevost H3-41 coaches in 1999.

Lakefront Lines of Cleveland, Ohio added 18 Prevost H3-45 coaches to its fleet in 1998. This H3-45 is seen on a tour in New York City in November 2001.

Chippewa Trails, of Chippewa Falls, Wisconsin, added this Prevost H3-45—one of the first to be delivered—to its fleet in 1994. Chippewa Trails is a charter and tour bus company and traces its origins to 1907.

Rimrock Stages of Billings, Montana added this Prevost H3-45 coach and two others to its fleet in 1999. The company also operates Prevost Le Mirage II coaches. Now a Trailways affiliate, Rimrock, which has a 30-year history, has a number of routes in Montana and also is a major charter and tour company in the area.

Burlington Trailways, West Burlington, Iowa, purchased this Prevost H3-45 in 1998. It has a galley and special passenger amenities and is referred to as a Five Star Coach in the Burlington fleet. Another similar coach was added in 1999.

This Prevost H3-45 coach was added to the fleet of Jonesboro, Arkansas-based Great Southern Coaches in 1999. Great Southern, an important charter and tour company in north-eastern Arkansas, purchased another similar Prevost coach in 2002.

Dillon's Bus Service, a Coach USA Company, of Baltimore and Millersville, Maryland recently added this Prevost H3-45 coach to its fleet. Dillon's, which has been in business since 1970, does extensive charter, tour, commuter and contract services.

Aerocar of Montreal, Quebec acquired six of these Prevost H3-40 coaches in 1992 for charter and tour services. Aerocar became a part of the Groupe Gaudreault organization in 1991 and has now been absorbed by Murray Hill, another Groupe Gaudreault member.

Prevost Car, Inc. recognized the value of flexibility in coach manufacturing a number of years ago. As a result, modifications can be made to the bodies of Prevost coaches to fit most any customer need. Pictured here is a Le Mirage XL coach for private use. Note the interesting treatment of the side windows, stainless steel siding and chromed wheels. The Prevost Le Mirage XL was first introduced for conversions in 1978.

Marathon Coach of Coburn, Oregon is one of the largest coach conversion companies in the world, if not the largest. Marathon specializes in using Prevost body shells. Shown here is a Prevost H3-40 coach with a luxury-interior VIP conversion by Marathon. Note that the coach has a raised roof, which Prevost incorporates into the shells.

Marathon Coach customized the interior of this Prevost H3-40 coach for a private motor home customer. The roof was raised, but side windows were retained at their normal heights.

Side windows on Prevost conversion coaches can be changed to suit customers' requirements. This Prevost H3-40 coach was customized by Marathon for a corporate customer, including the addition of a matching race-car trailer.

One of Prevost's H3-45 "Ultimate Class" conversion bus shells is shown here as converted to a luxury coach by Marathon Coach. In recent years Prevost has offered innovative technology for slide-out sections for the coaches, providing increased interior space in the front and rear. Marathon has furnished the interior with luxury amenities.

The 45-foot Prevost Le Mirage XL II coach can be provided with slide-out sections in the front and rear, resulting in a very roomy interior. Pictured here with the exterior of the coach and the slide-out extended is the luxury interior with its sofa, bar and other features. The coach has a raised roof and a modified front.

Attractive graphics for the exterior of converted coaches is another specialty by Marathon Coach. This Prevost Le Mirage XL II coach has stainless steel below the belt with the overall graphics. This coach incorporates features of both the Le Mirage XL II and H3-45 Prevost models. The interior has many amenities including a bar area. Detroit Diesel Series 60 diesel engines are standard on all Prevost coaches.

Pictured is a Prevost H3-45 coach converted by Marathon Coach, with the "Ultimate Class" slide-out sections in the front and rear. The interior reflects the designer fabrics, luxury leather and sculptured carpeting that Marathon offers. Prevost coaches for conversions have all the latest mechanical features including independent suspension systems for a comfortable, safe ride.

Le Robuste et Puissant INTERURBAIN

Les Ateliers Prévost INC.
SAINTE-CLAIRE   CTÉ. DORCHESTER, P.Q.

Les Ateliers Prevost, Inc. published one of the first brochures. It was distributed about 1946 and described the Prevost Interurban model buses.

City and suburban Prevost model buses produced in the late 1940s were presented in this brochure of Les Ateliers Prevost, Inc.

In 1954, this 18-page booklet described the Interurban model buses produced by Les Ateliers Prevost at that time.

In the mid-1950s the name Prevost Coach Co. was used for sales literature published in English. This piece described the 37-passenger Prevost Interurban model buses.

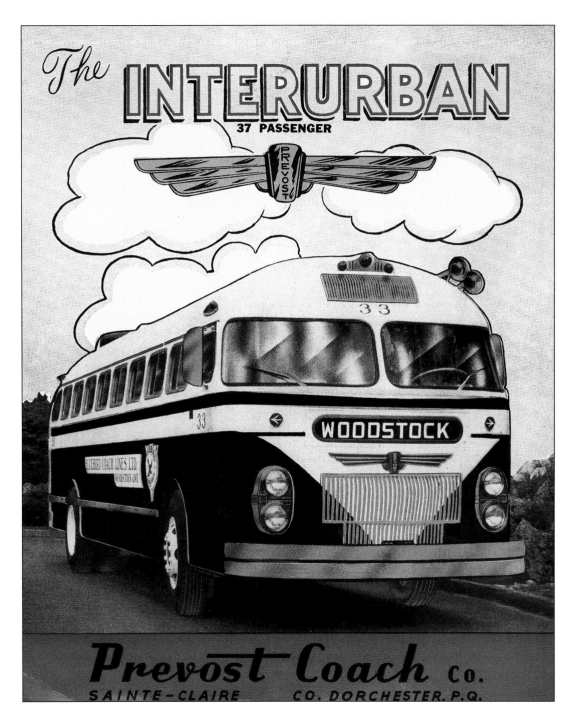

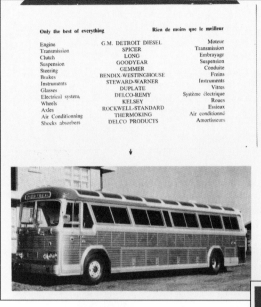

Only the best of everything   Rien de moins que le meilleur

Engine	G.M. DETROIT DIESEL	Moteur
Transmission	SPICER	Transmission
Clutch	LONG	Embrayage
Suspension	GOODYEAR	Suspension
Steering	GEMMER	Conduite
Brakes	BENDIX-WESTINGHOUSE	Freins
Instruments	STEWARD-WARNER	Instruments
Glasses	DUPLATE	Vitres
Electrical system	DELCO-REMY	Système électrique
Wheels	KELSEY	Roues
Axles	ROCKWELL-STANDARD	Essieux
Air Conditionning	THERMOKING	Air conditionné
Shocks absorbers	DELCO PRODUCTS	Amortisseurs

the / le SUPER-PANORAMIQUE
47 passengers - 47 passagers

Prevost's long experience and staff ability have permitted to incorporate with real success into this SUPER-PANORAMIQUE model such advanced design concepts as:

Aircraft type, "Instant Comfort" air conditionning and toilet,

Extra wide base air suspension,

Exclusive third axle design,

Double glazed tinted windows...

...and many "first" which places this bus in a class of its own!

Par une très longue expérience, Prevost a acquis dans le domaine de l'autobus la maîtrise technique, qui seule pouvait lui permettre d'incorporer dans ce SUPER-PANORAMIQUE des concepts avancés comme suit:

Système d'air conditionné à "confort instantanné" et toilette de types avion,

Suspension à voie très large,

Conception très nouvelle de l'essieu auxiliaire,

Fenêtres à vitres doubles et teintées...

... et nombres d'autres innovations qui le placent dans une catégorie à part.

The Prevost Panoramique and Super-Panoramique models were presented in this folder. The Travel Air model and a city bus were also introduced.

Summary Report on the Finest BUSSES

Présentation Sommaire des Meilleurs AUTOBUS

PREVOST CAR, Inc.   STE-CLAIRE, (DORCHESTER) P.Q.
418 - 645-3291   CANADA.

— Further informations on request —   — Renseignements supplémentaires sur demande —

THE / LE PANORAMIQUE

The outstanding experience accumulated over the years (since 1924) has resulted in this very modern model.

Both the operation performance and Passengers' reaction have confirmed the excellence of design and production.

This model is available with either two or three axels for 41, 45, 49 or 53 passengers.

L'expérience exceptionnelle acquise depuis 1924 a permis la conception et la production de cet autobus des plus modernes.

Ainsi un très haut degré d'excellence a été atteint tel que démontré à l'usage et par les réactions extrêmement favorables de la clientèle.

Ce model est disponible équipé soit de deux, soit de trois essieux, pour 41, 45, 49 ou 53 passagers.

A smaller and medium size multi-purpose bus. Suitable for transit, airport and feeder bus. From 19-passenger up to 33 passenger recliner in the larger option.

Cargo bus model with baggage compartment in rear.

Built to the same high quality standard of construction, suspension and interior decoration as the highway buses.

Petit modèle économique à usages multiples tel que; service d'aéroport, autobus supplémentaire; modèle jusqu'à 33 passagers, inclinable. Modèle avec grande chambre à baggage pour service de courrier.

Modèle pour service combiné passagers et express.

Construction, confort, suspension et finition aux mêmes normes que les autobus Interurbains modernes.

THE / LE TRAVELAIR

City Model
33 — 37 passengers

Modèle de Ville
33 — 37 passagers

The Champion, the first Prevost model to be marketed in the United States, was described in this 1968 sales brochure.

THE BUS INDUSTRY HAS A NEW

CHAMPION

by **PREVOST**

In 1976, the Prevost Le Mirage was introduced in this brochure, which also had information on the glass-top Astral coach and the Marathon model.

Prevost XL Le Mirage and Marathon model coaches were described in this 1984 brochure. The XL models were the first to have the 102-inch-wide bodies that had become the legal width for buses at that time.

PREVOST

THE 'ULTIMATE' CLASS

LeMIRAGE XL WITH iSs

The Prevost Independent Suspension System was one of the features of this sales piece produced especially for customers of motor homes and special coaches.

Treat Your People To A Million-Dollar Ride

FIRST WITH THE HIGHEST STANDINGS — The Prevost H-Series came first with the highest standings of all touring coaches in America. First and tallest high-decker with an all-stainless steel integral structure based on aerospace technology. First to boast a precision-molded fiber composite outer shell reinforced with carbon fiber and Kevlar in critical areas. First to include ABS as standard equipment. First with frameless flush-mounted privacy glass side windows (a Prevost patent). First and only touring coaches to offer the hallmark million-dollar ride of their sister flagship, the Prevost H3-45 VIP high-end motorhome conversion shell.

PROVEN TECHNOLOGY WITH STYLE — From their initial launch the Prevost H-Series were acclaimed as a quantum leap in passenger transportation by motorcoach. More than 15 years later, thanks to its superlative engineering capabilities, Prevost is still setting the pace with the kind of innovative product designs that creates industry benchmarks in state-of-the-art technology, proven dependability and safety, combined with the advanced styling and the superior riding comfort passengers truly appreciate.

PREVOST H-SERIES STAND A CUT ABOVE — Prevost H-Series premium touring coaches are built by the same people who take pride in their reputation as the world's leading manufacturer of the top-of-the-line PREVOST H3-45 VIP coach shells for 'Ultimate' Class motorhome and specialty conversions that reach well over a million when custom furbished.

PASSENGER-FRIENDLY ENTRANCEWAY — The entranceway on the H-Series is an integrated design concept that works in total harmony with human ergonomics. Both the shape and the offset of each step are designed to provide maximum stepping area, and streamlined soft-touch handrails are strategically positioned to provide reliable guidance for passengers and driver to securely ease in or out of the coach.

Both fiber composite staircase modules are surfaced with seamless anti-slip gelcoat for easier cleaning and maintenance. Reflective off-white borders trim the steps and lower sidewalls for added visibility and surefootedness. The new stairwell is lit with three recessed LEDs staggered along the lower sidewalls and with a halogen ceiling spot to create a warm welcoming atmosphere.

The largest full-color Prevost brochure announces the H-series coaches with large windshield, passenger-friendly entrance and other features.

A Word from the Author

My first look at Prevost buses came in 1950 when I traveled to Canada's Quebec province for the first time. I was employed by Jefferson Transportation Company at the time, and the trip to Quebec and back by bus was my vacation that year.

In Montreal, I first had a look at Prevost buses and I photographed a number of them while I visited that interesting city. In Quebec City I observed and photographed many Prevost buses. The Prevost factory was near Quebec City, although I did not visit it then. Quebec had many small intercity bus lines, and the Prevost buses on those lines reached most every village and city in the area.

Then, a couple of years later, I traveled to western Canada on vacation and saw some Prevost buses. In Edmonton, Alberta, I saw the Prevost city bus of Diamond Bus Lines, which was operating suburban service.

My first visit to the Prevost factory came in 1967. I had traveled to Quebec again and went to Ste.-Claire to visit the factory. I also attended the National Association of Motor Bus Owners (now American Bus Association) annual meeting in Montreal. There, the new Prevost Champion model was on display. Prevost was showing its new bus to a wider audience with the objective of selling buses to United States operators. It proved a good move for Prevost.

After I began publishing the bus industry trade journal Bus Ride, Prevost became one of the first regular advertisers. A very good relationship resulted, and I visited the Prevost factory many times over a number of years.

I also traveled on Prevost buses on many occasions. I continued to photograph Prevost buses during my travels and wrote articles about Prevost buses and about companies that operated them.

I also had the opportunity to meet many people in the Prevost organization, and good friendships were established.

I recall attending the unveiling of the articulated Prevost H5-60 coach, and I had the opportunity to ride this new Prevost model on several occasions. Whenever new Prevost models were introduced, I was usually present to see, ride, photograph and write about them. The excellent relationship I have had with Prevost has always been very special to me.

Prevost Car, Inc. has shown leadership over the years by recognizing the opportunity to produce specialized bus bodies for private individuals and business firms. In addition, new motorcoach designs for operators of intercity, charter and tour services have been introduced appropriately when opportunities arose.

It has been a pleasure to produce this book on the buses of Prevost Car. The cooperation from the Prevost people has been very generous. I especially wish to thank Paul Leger, president of the Bus History Association in Halifax, Nova Scotia and Jean Breton, Charlesbourg, Quebec, for sharing many photographs and information used in this book.

The book Bus Industry Chronicle, which I recently authored, contains more information and pictures about Prevost.

Additional bus industry history has been recorded in several other Photo Archive books I have authored or co-authored. These books are: *Greyhound Buses 1914-2000 Photo Archive, Trailways Buses 1936-2001 Photo Archive, Yellow Coach Buses 1923-1943 Photo Archive, Trolley Buses 1913-2001 Photo Archive* and *Fageol & Twin Coach Buses 1922-1956 Photo Archive.*

William A. Luke, the author of this book, stands between George Bourelle (left), President of Prevost Car, Inc. and Robert Wood, Chairman of Prevost Car, Inc. Behind them is the new Prevost H3-45 2003 coach.

126

MORE TITLES FROM ICONOGRAFIX

AMERICAN CULTURE

- *COCA-COLA: A HISTORY IN PHOTOGRAPHS 1930-1969* ISBN 1-882256-46-8
- *COCA-COLA: ITS VEHICLES IN PHOTOGRAPHS 1930-1969* ISBN 1-882256-47-6
- *PHILLIPS 66 1945-1954 PHOTO ARCHIVE* ISBN 1-882256-42-5

AUTOMOTIVE

- *AMX PHOTO ARCHIVE: FROM CONCEPT TO REALITY* ISBN 1-58388-062-3
- *CAMARO 1967-2000 PHOTO ARCHIVE* ISBN 1-58388-032-1
- *CHEVROLET STATION WAGONS 1946-1966 PHOTO ARCHIVE* ISBN 1-58388-069-0
- *CLASSIC AMERICAN LIMOUSINES 1955-2000 PHOTO ARCHIVE* ISBN 1-58388-041-0
- *CORVAIR by CHEVROLET EXP. & PROD. CARS 1957-1969 LUDVIGSEN LIBRARY SERIES* ISBN 1-58388-058-5
- *CORVETTE THE EXOTIC EXPERIMENTAL CARS, LUDVIGSEN LIBRARY SERIES* ISBN 1-58388-017-8
- *CORVETTE PROTOTYPES & SHOW CARS PHOTO ALBUM* ISBN 1-882256-77-8
- *EARLY FORD V-8s 1932-1942 PHOTO ALBUM* ISBN 1-882256-97-2
- *FORD POSTWAR FLATHEADS 1946-1953 PHOTO ARCHIVE* ISBN 1-58388-080-1
- *IMPERIAL 1955-1963 PHOTO ARCHIVE* ISBN 1-882256-22-0
- *IMPERIAL 1964-1968 PHOTO ARCHIVE* ISBN 1-882256-23-9
- *JAVELIN PHOTO ARCHIVE: FROM CONCEPT TO REALITY* ISBN 1-58388-071-2
- *LINCOLN MOTOR CARS 1920-1942 PHOTO ARCHIVE* ISBN 1-882256-57-3
- *LINCOLN MOTOR CARS 1946-1960 PHOTO ARCHIVE* ISBN 1-882256-58-1
- *PACKARD MOTOR CARS 1935-1942 PHOTO ARCHIVE* ISBN 1-882256-44-1
- *PACKARD MOTOR CARS 1946-1958 PHOTO ARCHIVE* ISBN 1-882256-45-X
- *PONTIAC DREAM CARS, SHOW CARS & PROTOTYPES 1928-1998 PHOTO ALBUM* ISBN 1-882256-93-X
- *PONTIAC FIREBIRD TRANS-AM 1969-1999 PHOTO ALBUM* ISBN 1-882256-95-6
- *PONTIAC FIREBIRD 1967-2000 PHOTO HISTORY* ISBN 1-58388-028-3
- *RAMBLER 1950-1969 PHOTO ARCHIVE* ISBN 1-58388-078-X
- *STRETCH LIMOUSINES 1928-2001 PHOTO ARCHIVE* ISBN 1-58388-070-4
- *STUDEBAKER 1933-1942 PHOTO ARCHIVE* ISBN 1-882256-24-7
- *ULTIMATE CORVETTE TRIVIA CHALLENGE* ISBN 1-58388-035-6

BUSES

- *BUSES OF MOTOR COACH INDUSTRIES 1932-2000 PHOTO ARCHIVE* ISBN 1-58388-039-9
- *FAGEOL & TWIN COACH BUSES 1922-1956 PHOTO ARCHIVE* ISBN 1-58388-075-5
- *FLXIBLE TRANSIT BUSES 1953-1995 PHOTO ARCHIVE* ISBN 1-58388-053-4
- *GREYHOUND BUSES 1914-2000 PHOTO ARCHIVE* ISBN 1-58388-027-5
- *MACK® BUSES 1900-1960 PHOTO ARCHIVE** ISBN 1-58388-020-8
- *PREVOST BUSES 1924-2002 PHOTO ARCHIVE* ISBN 1-58388-083-6
- *TRAILWAYS BUSES 1936-2001 PHOTO ARCHIVE* ISBN 1-58388-029-1
- *TROLLEY BUSES 1913-2001 PHOTO ARCHIVE* ISBN 1-58388-057-7
- *YELLOW COACH BUSES 1923-1943 PHOTO ARCHIVE* ISBN 1-58388-054-2

EMERGENCY VEHICLES

- *AMERICAN AMBULANCE 1900-2002: AN ILLUSTRATED HISTORY* ISBN 1-58388-081-X
- *AMERICAN LAFRANCE 700 SERIES 1945-1952 PHOTO ARCHIVE* ISBN 1-882256-90-5
- *AMERICAN LAFRANCE 700 SERIES 1945-1952 PHOTO ARCHIVE VOLUME 2* ISBN 1-58388-025-9
- *AMERICAN LAFRANCE 700 & 800 SERIES 1953-1958 PHOTO ARCHIVE* ISBN 1-882256-91-3
- *AMERICAN LAFRANCE 900 SERIES 1958-1964 PHOTO ARCHIVE* ISBN 1-58388-002-X
- *CLASSIC SEAGRAVE 1935-1951 PHOTO ARCHIVE* ISBN 1-58388-034-8
- *CROWN FIRECOACH 1951-1985 PHOTO ARCHIVE* ISBN 1-58388-047-X
- *FIRE CHIEF CARS 1900-1997 PHOTO ALBUM* ISBN 1-882256-87-5
- *HAHN FIRE APPARATUS 1923-1990 PHOTO ARCHIVE* ISBN 1-58388-077-1
- *HEAVY RESCUE TRUCKS 1931-2000 PHOTO GALLERY* ISBN 1-58388-045-3
- *INDUSTRIAL AND PRIVATE FIRE APPARATUS 1925-2001 PHOTO ARCHIVE* ISBN 1-58388-049-6
- *LOS ANGELES CITY FIRE APPARATUS 1953-1999 PHOTO ARCHIVE* ISBN 1-58388-012-7
- *MACK MODEL C FIRE TRUCKS 1957-1967 PHOTO ARCHIVE** ISBN 1-58388-014-3
- *MACK MODEL L FIRE TRUCKS 1940-1954 PHOTO ARCHIVE** ISBN 1-882256-86-7
- *MAXIM FIRE APPARATUS 1914-1989 PHOTO ARCHIVE* ISBN 1-58388-050-X
- *NAVY & MARINE CORPS FIRE APPARATUS 1836 -2000 PHOTO GALLERY* ISBN 1-58388-031-3
- *PIERRE THIBAULT LTD. FIRE APPARATUS 1918-1990 PHOTO ARCHIVE* ISBN 1-58388-074-7
- *PIRSCH FIRE APPARATUS 1890-1991 PHOTO ARCHIVE* ISBN 1-58388-082-8
- *POLICE CARS: RESTORING, COLLECTING & SHOWING AMERICA'S FINEST SEDANS* ISBN 1-58388-046-1
- *SEAGRAVE 70TH ANNIVERSARY SERIES PHOTO ARCHIVE* ISBN 1-58388-001-1
- *TASC FIRE APPARATUS 1946-1985 PHOTO ARCHIVE* ISBN 1-58388-065-8
- *VOLUNTEER & RURAL FIRE APPARATUS PHOTO GALLERY* ISBN 1-58388-005-4
- *W.S. DARLEY & CO. FIRE APPARATUS 1908-2000 PHOTO ARCHIVE* ISBN 1-58388-061-5
- *WARD LAFRANCE FIRE TRUCKS 1918-1978 PHOTO ARCHIVE* ISBN 1-58388-013-5
- *WILDLAND FIRE APPARATUS 1940-2001 PHOTO GALLERY* ISBN 1-58388-056-9
- *YOUNG FIRE EQUIPMENT 1932-1991 PHOTO ARCHIVE* ISBN 1-58388-015-1

RACING

- *CHAPARRAL CAN-AM RACING CARS FROM TEXAS LUDVIGSEN LIBRARY SERIES* ISBN 1-58388-066-6
- *DRAG RACING FUNNY CARS OF THE 1970s PHOTO ARCHIVE* ISBN 1-58388-068-2
- *EL MIRAGE IMPRESSIONS: DRY LAKES LAND SPEED RACING* ISBN 1-58388-059-3
- *GT40 PHOTO ARCHIVE* ISBN 1-882256-64-6
- *INDY CARS OF THE 1950s, LUDVIGSEN LIBRARY SERIES* ISBN 1-58388-018-6
- *INDY CARS OF THE 1960s, LUDVIGSEN LIBRARY SERIES* ISBN 1-58388-052-6
- *INDIANAPOLIS RACING CARS OF FRANK KURTIS 1941-1963 PHOTO ARCHIVE* ISBN 1-58388-026-7
- *JUAN MANUEL FANGIO WORLD CHAMPION DRIVER SERIES PHOTO ALBUM* ISBN 1-58388-008-9
- *MARIO ANDRETTI WORLD CHAMPION DRIVER SERIES PHOTO ALBUM* ISBN 1-58388-009-7
- *MERCEDES-BENZ 300SL RACING CARS 1952-1953 LUDVIGSEN LIBRARY SERIES* ISBN 1-58388-067-4
- *NOVI V-8 INDY CARS 1941-1965 LUDVIGSEN LIBRARY SERIES* ISBN 1-58388-037-2
- *SEBRING 12-HOUR RACE 1970 PHOTO ARCHIVE* ISBN 1-882256-20-4
- *VANDERBILT CUP RACE 1936 & 1937 PHOTO ARCHIVE* ISBN 1-882256-66-2

RAILWAYS

- *CHICAGO, ST. PAUL, MINNEAPOLIS & OMAHA RAILWAY 1880-1940 PHOTO ARCHIVE* ISBN 1-882256-67-0
- *CHICAGO & NORTH WESTERN RAILWAY 1975-1995 PHOTO ARCHIVE* ISBN 1-882256-76-X
- *GREAT NORTHERN RAILWAY 1945-1970 VOL 2 PHOTO ARCHIVE* ISBN 1-882256-79-4
- *GREAT NORTHERN RAILWAY ORE DOCKS OF LAKE SUPERIOR PHOTO ARCHIVE* ISBN 1-58388-073-9
- *ILLINOIS CENTRAL RAILROAD 1854-1960 PHOTO ARCHIVE* ISBN 1-58388-063-1
- *MILWAUKEE ROAD 1850-1960 PHOTO ARCHIVE* ISBN 1-882256-61-1
- *MILWAUKEE ROAD DEPOTS 1856-1954 PHOTO ARCHIVE* ISBN 1-58388-040-2
- *SHOW TRAINS OF THE 20TH CENTURY* ISBN 1-58388-030-5
- *SOO LINE 1975-1992 PHOTO ARCHIVE* ISBN 1-882256-68-9
- *TRAINS OF THE TWIN PORTS, DULUTH-SUPERIOR IN THE 1950s PHOTO ARCHIVE* ISBN 1-58388-003-8
- *TRAINS OF THE CIRCUS 1872-1956* ISBN 1-58388-024-0
- *TRAINS of the UPPER MIDWEST PHOTO ARCHIVE STEAM&DIESEL in the1950s &1960s* ISBN 1-58388-036-4
- *WISCONSIN CENTRAL LIMITED 1987-1996 PHOTO ARCHIVE* ISBN 1-882256-75-1
- *WISCONSIN CENTRAL RAILWAY 1871-1909 PHOTO ARCHIVE* ISBN 1-882256-78-6

TRUCKS

- *AUTOCAR TRUCKS 1950-1987 PHOTO ARCHIVE* ISBN 1-58388-072-0
- *BEVERAGE TRUCKS 1910-1975 PHOTO ARCHIVE* ISBN 1-882256-60-3
- *BROCKWAY TRUCKS 1948-1961 PHOTO ARCHIVE** ISBN 1-882256-55-7
- *CHEVROLET EL CAMINO PHOTO HISTORY INCL GMC SPRINT & CABALLERO* ISBN 1-58388-044-5
- *CIRCUS AND CARNIVAL TRUCKS 1923-2000 PHOTO ARCHIVE* ISBN 1-58388-048-8
- *DODGE PICKUPS 1939-1978 PHOTO ALBUM* ISBN 1-882256-82-4
- *DODGE POWER WAGONS 1940-1980 PHOTO ARCHIVE* ISBN 1-882256-89-1
- *DODGE POWER WAGON PHOTO HISTORY* ISBN 1-58388-019-4
- *DODGE RAM TRUCKS 1994-2001 PHOTO HISTORY* ISBN 1-58388-051-8
- *DODGE TRUCKS 1929-1947 PHOTO ARCHIVE* ISBN 1-882256-36-0
- *DODGE TRUCKS 1948-1960 PHOTO ARCHIVE* ISBN 1-882256-37-9
- *FORD 4X4s 1935-1990 PHOTO HISTORY* ISBN 1-58388-079-8
- *FORD HEAVY-DUTY TRUCKS 1948-1998 PHOTO HISTORY* ISBN 1-58388-043-7
- *JEEP 1941-2000 PHOTO ARCHIVE* ISBN 1-58388-021-6
- *JEEP PROTOTYPES & CONCEPT VEHICLES PHOTO ARCHIVE* ISBN 1-58388-033-X
- *MACK MODEL AB PHOTO ARCHIVE** ISBN 1-882256-18-2
- *MACK AP SUPER-DUTY TRUCKS 1926-1938 PHOTO ARCHIVE** ISBN 1-882256-54-9
- *MACK MODEL B 1953-1966 VOL 2 PHOTO ARCHIVE** ISBN 1-882256-34-4
- *MACK EB-EC-ED-EE-EF-EG-DE 1936-1951 PHOTO ARCHIVE** ISBN 1-882256-29-8
- *MACK EH-EJ-EM-EQ-ER-ES 1936-1950 PHOTO ARCHIVE** ISBN 1-882256-39-5
- *MACK FC-FCSW-NW 1936-1947 PHOTO ARCHIVE** ISBN 1-882256-28-X
- *MACK FG-FH-FJ-FK-FN-FP-FT-FW 1937-1950 PHOTO ARCHIVE** ISBN 1-882256-35-2
- *MACK LF-LH-LJ-LM-LT 1940-1956 PHOTO ARCHIVE** ISBN 1-882256-38-7
- *MACK TRUCKS PHOTO GALLERY** ISBN 1-882256-88-3
- *NEW CAR CARRIERS 1910-1998 PHOTO ALBUM* ISBN 1-882256-98-0
- *PLYMOUTH COMMERCIAL VEHICLES PHOTO ARCHIVE* ISBN 1-58388-004-6
- *REFUSE TRUCKS PHOTO ARCHIVE* ISBN 1-58388-042-9
- *RVs & CAMPERS 1900-2000: AN ILLUSTRATED HISTORY* ISBN 1-58388-064-X
- *STUDEBAKER TRUCKS 1927-1940 PHOTO ARCHIVE* ISBN 1-882256-40-9
- *WHITE TRUCKS 1900-1937 PHOTO ARCHIVE* ISBN 1-882256-80-8

TRACTORS & CONSTRUCTION EQUIPMENT

- *CASE TRACTORS 1912-1959 PHOTO ARCHIVE* ISBN 1-882256-32-8
- *CATERPILLAR PHOTO GALLERY* ISBN 1-882256-70-0
- *CATERPILLAR POCKET GUIDE THE TRACK-TYPE TRACTORS 1925-1957* ISBN 1-58388-022-4
- *CATERPILLAR D-2 & R-2 PHOTO ARCHIVE* ISBN 1-882256-99-9
- *CATERPILLAR D-8 1933-1974 PHOTO ARCHIVE INCLUDING DIESEL 75 & RD-8* ISBN 1-882256-96-4
- *CATERPILLAR MILITARY TRACTORS VOLUME 1 PHOTO ARCHIVE* ISBN 1-882256-16-6
- *CATERPILLAR MILITARY TRACTORS VOLUME 2 PHOTO ARCHIVE* ISBN 1-882256-17-4
- *CATERPILLAR SIXTY PHOTO ARCHIVE* ISBN 1-882256-05-0
- *CATERPILLAR TEN PHOTO ARCHIVE INCLUDING 7C FIFTEEN & HIGH FIFTEEN* ISBN 1-58388-011-9
- *CATERPILLAR THIRTY PHOTO ARCHIVE 2ND ED. INC. BEST THIRTY, 6G THIRTY & R-4* ISBN 1-58388-006-2
- *CIRCUS & CARNIVAL TRACTORS 1930-2001 PHOTO ARCHIVE* ISBN 1-58388-076-3
- *CLETRAC AND OLIVER CRAWLERS PHOTO ARCHIVE* ISBN 1-882256-43-3
- *CLASSIC AMERICAN STEAMROLLERS 1871-1935 PHOTO ARCHIVE* ISBN 1-58388-038-0
- *FARMALL CUB PHOTO ARCHIVE* ISBN 1-882256-71-9
- *FARMALL F- SERIES PHOTO ARCHIVE* ISBN 1-882256-02-6
- *FARMALL MODEL H PHOTO ARCHIVE* ISBN 1-882256-03-4
- *FARMALL MODEL M PHOTO ARCHIVE* ISBN 1-882256-15-8
- *FARMALL REGULAR PHOTO ARCHIVE* ISBN 1-882256-14-X
- *FARMALL SUPER SERIES PHOTO ARCHIVE* ISBN 1-882256-49-2
- *FORDSON 1917-1928 PHOTO ARCHIVE* ISBN 1-882256-33-6
- *HART-PARR PHOTO ARCHIVE* ISBN 1-882256-08-5
- *HOLT TRACTORS PHOTO ARCHIVE* ISBN 1-882256-10-7
- *INTERNATIONAL TRACTRACTOR PHOTO ARCHIVE* ISBN 1-882256-48-4
- *JOHN DEERE MODEL A PHOTO ARCHIVE* ISBN 1-882256-12-3
- *JOHN DEERE MODEL D PHOTO ARCHIVE* ISBN 1-882256-00-X
- *MARION CONSTRUCTION MACHINERY 1884-1975 PHOTO ARCHIVE* ISBN 1-58388-060-7
- *OLIVER TRACTORS PHOTO ARCHIVE* ISBN 1-882256-09-3
- *RUSSELL GRADERS PHOTO ARCHIVE* ISBN 1-882256-11-5
- *TWIN CITY TRACTOR PHOTO ARCHIVE* ISBN 1-882256-06-9

*This product is sold under license from Mack Trucks, Inc. Mack is a registered Trademark of Mack Trucks, Inc. All rights reserved.

All Iconografix books are available from direct mail specialty book dealers and bookstores worldwide, or can be ordered from the publisher. For book trade and distribution information or to add your name to our mailing list and receive a **FREE CATALOG** contact:

Iconografix, PO Box 446, Dept BK, Hudson, Wisconsin, 54016   Telephone: (715) 381-9755, (800) 289-3504 (USA), Fax: (715) 381-9756

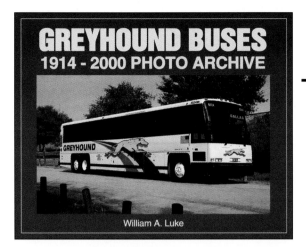
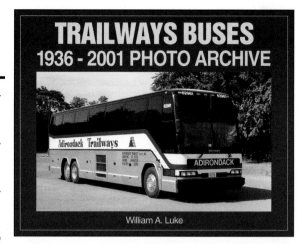
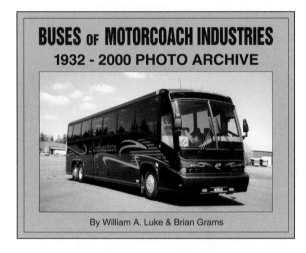
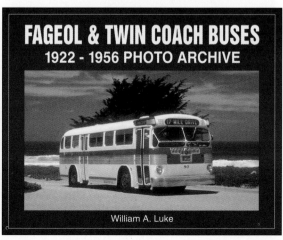
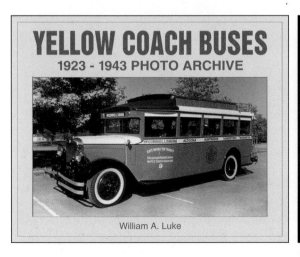
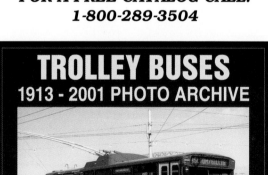
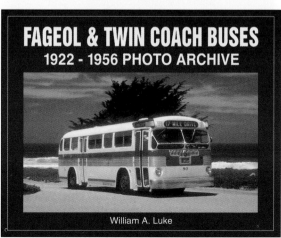